THE NUTCRACKE

CHRISTMAS COLORI

THIS BOOK BELONG TO

THE NUTCRACKER BALLET
COLORING BOOK

Test color page

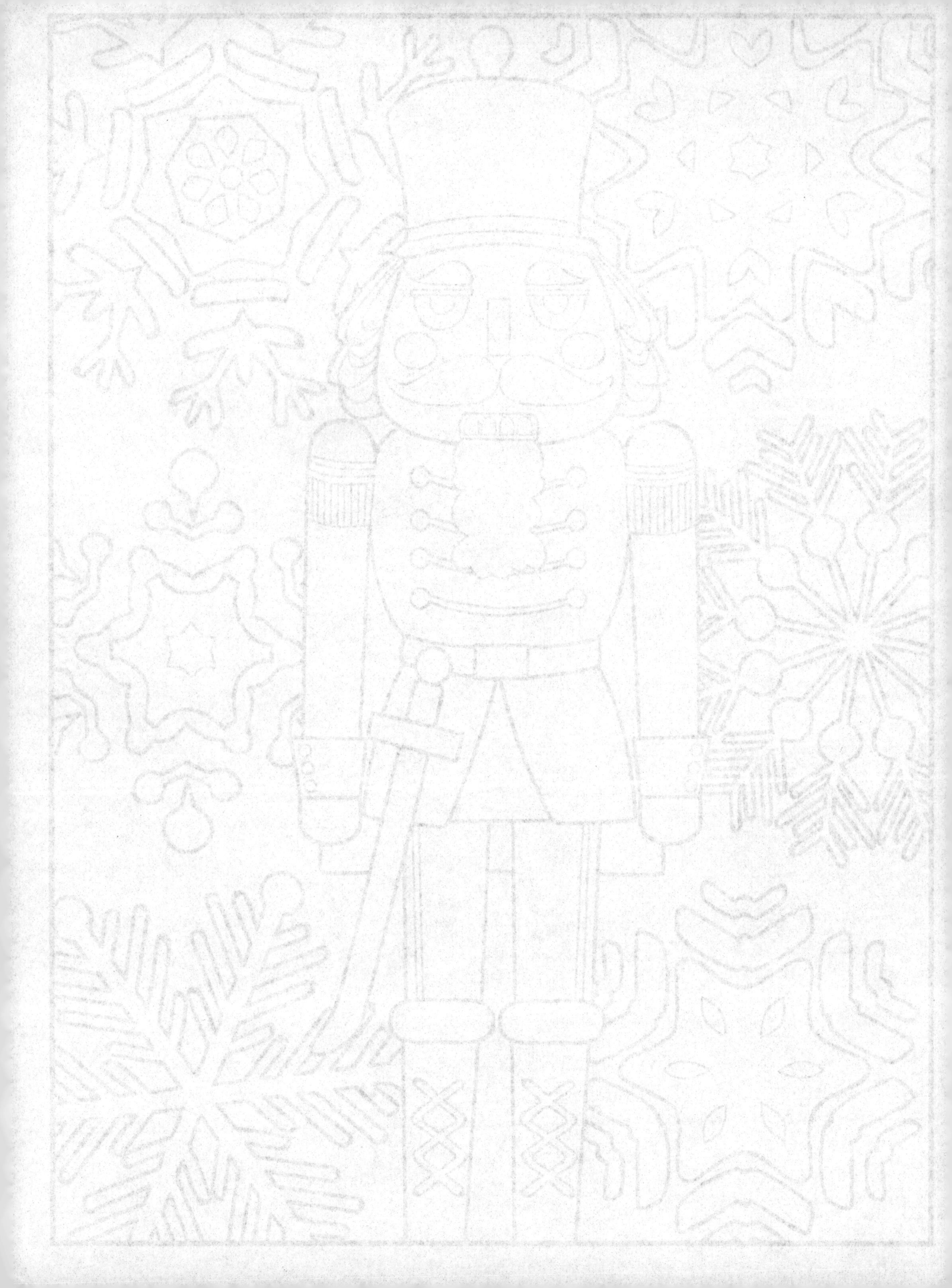

THANK YOU VERY MUCH
FOR TRUSTING AND CHOOSING
OUR PRODUCT

WISH YOU ALL THE BEST
IN YOUR FUTURE

HOPE YOU WILL PUT YOUR TRUST
IN OUR NEXT PRODUCT

WRITE DOWN
WHAT YOU LIKE ABOUT THIS BOOK:

....

....

....

....

....

....

....

....

....

....

....

....

....

Made in the USA
Columbia, SC
16 December 2024

49479364R00037